The Artistic Revolution: Unleashing Creativity with AI Art

Max Revene

Contents

Chapter One

What is AI Art?

The world of art has always been a bastion of creativity, innovation, and imagination. However, the recent advancements in artificial intelligence (AI) have opened up new possibilities for artists and creative minds alike. AI art is the latest buzzword in the art industry, and it is rapidly changing the way we perceive and create art. While some people may view AI-generated art as a threat to traditional artistic methods, it can actually complement and enhance human creativity. In this chapter, we will explore the benefits of using AI in art creation and how it can unleash your inner artist. We will also delve into the ethical implications of AI-generated art and highlight some success stories of artists who have embraced this technology to produce stunning works of art.

WHAT IS AI ART? UNDERSTANDING THE BASICS

Artificial Intelligence (AI) can be defined as the development of computer systems that can perform tasks that normally require human intelligence, such as language recognition, decision-making, and image recognition. When it comes to AI art, it is a subset of generative art where algorithms are used to create unique and original artwork. In other words, AI is trained to generate images based on certain inputs. One of the defining features of AI art is its ability to create works that are unpredictable and unique. Unlike traditional art forms where artists have complete control over the creative process, algorithms in AI art introduce an element of randomness that can lead to surprising results. This quality makes AI-generated work fascinating not only for viewers but also for artists themselves who can be surprised by their own creations. Another notable aspect of AI art is its reliance on deep learning neural networks.

These networks are trained using large datasets of images and text corpus and develop an understanding of styles, patterns, and visual cues in order to create new works. The more data fed into these systems, the more accurate they become at generating new images. AI-generated artwork has garnered significant attention in recent years due to its innovative approach and potential for creativity. While some critics argue that it lacks human emotion or consciousness, others point out that this very feature sets it apart from traditional artworks. Overall, understanding what constitutes AI-generated art depends on recognizing the role played by algorithms in creating unique pieces. By relying on deep learning neural networks trained with vast amounts of data sets that learn about specific visual themes or motifs over time – such as colors or shapes – we can generate a whole new world of visual experiences through computer programs designed specifically for this purpose!

AI ART FROM TEXT PROMPTS

One of the most fascinating and exciting aspects of AI art is the potential for collaboration between humans and machines. While algorithms can generate highly complex and intricate designs, they lack the creativity and intuition that comes naturally to artists. This is where "**prompts**" come in - a way to guide AI systems towards creative solutions while still allowing room for human input. The first step in creating an AI art prompt is establishing a clear goal or concept. Whether it's exploring a specific theme, experimenting with different styles or techniques, or simply generating novel visual ideas, having a specific starting point can help focus your AI algorithm towards a specific outcome.

It's important to consider how much control you want over the final output. Some prompts may involve setting strict parameters around color schemes, shapes, or textures, while others may allow for more randomization and experimentation. Depending on your goals and preferences as an artist, you'll want to experiment with different methods until you find one that works best for you. Finally, don't be afraid to get experimental! One of the biggest advantages of using AI in art is its ability to generate unexpected results that push boundaries and challenge our preconceptions of what constitutes "good" or "bad" art. By embracing randomness and risk-taking in your prompts, you may discover new approaches or techniques that can inspire future works.

UNDERSTANDING ALGORITHMS IN AI ART

Artificial intelligence has revolutionized the way art is created, and algorithms play a crucial role in generating these works of art. In AI art, algorithms refer to a set of mathematical rules that determine how an image or artwork is created. These rules are programmed into the computer system and guide the software to create unique and original pieces of art. One of the most popular types of algorithm in AI art is Generative Adversarial Networks (GANs). GANs use two neural networks to generate an image. The first network generates images in response to random input, while the second network assesses these images for their quality and authenticity. The two networks interact with each other until a realistic image is produced. Another type of algorithm used in AI art is Style Transfer.

Style transfer refers to a process where an algorithm can take the style from one image and apply it to another image. This technique can create interesting and unique artworks by blending different styles together. It's also important to understand that algorithms are not just limited to creating static images or digital paintings. They can be used in creating 3D animations, videos, and other multimedia content as well. The use of algorithms has opened up endless possibilities for artists and designers who want to create truly unique pieces that would have been impossible without artificial intelligence. By understanding how algorithms work in AI-generated art, we can appreciate the complexity of these creations while also embracing their limitless potential.

AI art is a rapidly expanding field that offers limitless potential for creativity and innovation. With its ability to learn and adapt, AI technology has the potential to revolutionize the way we create and experience art. Whether it's generative art, style transfer, or other forms of AI-generated content, there is no doubt that this technology will continue to have a significant impact on the world of art in the years to come. As we move forward into the future, it will be exciting to see how artists leverage this technology to push boundaries and inspire new forms of expression. In the future, we can expect to see AI art continue to evolve and create new possibilities for art and technology to intersect.

Chapter Two

History and Types of AI Art Technology

AI ART: EARLY HISTORY

Artificial Intelligence (AI) has been impacting art for decades. The evolution of AI Art can be traced back to the 1960s when computer-generated art first appeared on the scene. However, the term "AI Art" only gained recognition in the mid-2010s, around a decade after Nathan Myhrvold and his team at Microsoft Research organized the first exhibition of computer-generated art in Paris. During the early years, early pioneers like Vera Molnar, Michael Noll and Frieder Nake explored ways to use computers to create art. Their work paved the way for others like John Whitney who made significant strides in motion graphics using computers. However, these were mostly static images with limited artistic expressions.

The next significant milestone came in 1993 with Harold Cohen's "AARON", an AI program that generated original artistic compositions by interpreting visual patterns and abstract concepts. AARON spawned a new era of AI Art that promised more sophisticated algorithms for creating new works of art. In recent years, artists have continued to explore AI as a tool for creating new forms of expression including generative art made possible by deep learning neural networks and style transfer techniques pioneered by Gatys et al., which allow artists to combine different styles from different artworks into something entirely new.

AI ART: LATER HISTORY

Early Generative Art

Generative art has been around for decades, but it was only in recent years that artificial intelligence (AI) technology has enabled it to reach new heights. The concept of generative art involves using algorithms and computer processes to create unique, complex designs and images. While initially implemented with simple shapes and lines, the technology has since evolved into producing highly detailed and intricate artwork. The first examples of generative art date back to the 1960s, when artists began exploring the use of computers in creative expression. One such artist was Vera Molnar, who created geometric patterns using a plotter – a device that uses precise pen movements to create images on paper. Over time, advancements in computer graphics allowed for more sophisticated generative art techniques.

In the 1980s and 1990s, artists began experimenting with fractals – mathematical patterns that repeat themselves at different scales. This technique created complex designs that were impossible to replicate by hand. Later on, came evolutionary algorithms and swarm intelligence systems which enabled computers to generate unique designs based on feedback from previous iterations.

Fast forward to today and we have advanced deep-learning models like DALL-E which can generate incredibly realistic images from textual prompts. With this new technology, AI-generated artwork is becoming more lifelike than ever before – blurring the lines between what is real and what is generated by machines. One prominent example of generative art is the work of **Joshua Davis**, who uses software called Processing to create dynamic designs that evolve over time. His pieces blur the line between static image and interactive experience, inviting viewers to engage with them in new ways. Another notable figure in this field is **Golan Levin**, whose software-based installations explore themes like emergence, complexity, and pattern formation. Levin's work often involves live data feeds or input from sensors in the environment, making his pieces even more dynamic and unpredictable. Generative art challenges traditional notions of authorship and control in artistic creation. By embracing randomness and emergent behavior, these artists are pushing boundaries and opening up new possibilities for creative expression.

GANs

In recent years, the field of artificial intelligence has made significant strides in the realm of art. One of the most exciting developments is **generative adversarial networks**, or **GANs** for short. This chapter will explore what GANs are and how they work, as well as some notable examples of impressive artworks created using this technique. At its core, a GAN is a type of neural network that can generate new data that is similar to a given dataset. The network is composed of two parts: a generator and a discriminator. The generator creates new data based on input from random noise signals, while the discriminator evaluates whether that data resembles real examples from the dataset or not.

The training process for a GAN involves pitting these two parts against each other in an adversarial manner. The generator tries to create new data that will fool the discriminator into thinking it's real, while the discriminator tries to correctly identify which images are generated and which are real. One impressive example of artwork created using GANs is "**Portrait AI**," by **Robbie Barrat**. This project involved training several different GANs on various datasets of portraits from different time periods and styles. The resulting output was an entirely new set of portraits that blended elements from multiple styles seamlessly.

Another notable example is "**AICAN**," by **Ahmed Elgammal** at Rutgers University. AICAN used deep learning algorithms to analyze over 80,000 works of art spanning several centuries and genres before creating its own original pieces with no human intervention whatsoever. While these examples showcase just how powerful GANs can be in generating original artwork, there are also concerns surrounding their use in creating counterfeit art or even deep fakes. As with any technology, there are ethical implications that must be considered when utilizing it for creative purposes. Despite these concerns, it's clear that generative adversarial networks have opened up exciting possibilities for artists and creators alike. Whether it's creating entirely new works of art or augmenting existing pieces, GANs are sure to play a significant role in the future of AI-generated art.

Style Transfer

Style transfer is one of the most exciting techniques used in creating AI-generated art. It allows artists to transform an image into a different style while still retaining its original content. In this chapter, we will explore what style transfer is and how it works. At its core, style transfer involves separating a content image from a style image. The content image is the picture that the artist wants to transform, while the style image contains specific stylistic features that will be applied to the content image. The algorithm then extracts certain features from both images and combines them to create a new image.

One of the most popular methods for performing style transfer is called **neural-style transfer**. This method involves using convolutional neural networks (CNNs) to extract features from both images. Then, these features are combined using Gram matrices, which capture the correlations between different feature maps. Another popular method for performing style transfer is called adversarial-style transfer. This method involves using generative adversarial networks (GANs) to generate new images that blend together both styles and content in an entirely novel way. The results of style transfer can be truly astounding. For example, artists can use this technique to transform photographs into paintings by applying a particular painting's characteristic brushstrokes or color palette to it. Additionally, artists can use this technique to create entirely new works of art by mixing elements from different styles together.

One notable example of this technique being used in practice is **Google's DeepDream** algorithm. The algorithm uses CNNs trained on thousands of images and applies them recursively across an input image, resulting in trippy visuals reminiscent of Salvador Dali's surrealist artwork. However, there are some limitations when it comes to using style transfer for AI-generated art. One significant drawback is that current algorithms tend only to work well with simple shapes and patterns such as clouds or flowers; they struggle with more complex details such as faces or intricate architecture. Another drawback is that style transfer requires a considerable amount of processing power, which can make it difficult for artists without access to high-end hardware.

TEXT PROMPT GENERATIVE AI ART

Generative AI art has come a long way since its early days of producing simple geometric shapes and color combinations. The world of art has been revolutionized by the latest advancements in AI technology. From GANs to style transfer, artists now have access to a range of tools that enable them to create stunning works of art like never before. But one area where AI truly shines is in text prompt generative art, which uses natural language processing and machine learning algorithms to generate images based on textual input. Today, with the help of advanced algorithms and neural networks, generative AI art can produce stunning images that are both realistic and surreal. And all of this is possible with just a few lines of text as input.

The creative power of generative AI art lies in its ability to interpret text prompts and generate images that match the description. For example, if you provide a text prompt that says "a red apple on a wooden table," the algorithm will generate an image that depicts exactly what was described. However, it doesn't just stop there - the algorithm has the ability to add its own twists and interpretations to make the image even more interesting. One fascinating aspect of this technology is how it can be used to create images that humans might not have thought of themselves. By interpreting text prompts in unique ways, generative AI art can produce stunning visualizations that are both captivating and thought-provoking. Another aspect worth considering is how accessible this technology has become. With tools like DALL-E, anyone can create their own generative AI artwork by inputting simple text descriptions into a user-friendly interface.

This means that artists who might not have had access to expensive software or hardware can now experiment with creating their own unique pieces. In summary, from simple lines to complex designs, generative AI art has evolved dramatically over time thanks to advances in machine learning algorithms and neural networks. The creative power lies in its ability to interpret text prompts in unique ways that often result in stunning visuals that we may not have imagined ourselves.

Let's take a closer look at some of the most exciting developments in this field, including Midjourney, DALL-E, Diffusion and Leonar do.ai. We will explore how these technologies work.

Midjourney

Midjourney is a text-to-image generation system that uses natural language processing and deep learning algorithms to create photorealistic images from textual descriptions. It was developed by researchers at Adobe Research and UC Berkeley, and it has already produced some stunning results. During the 1980s, generative art began to take shape as artists experimented with computer programs to generate images. However, this art form did not receive worldwide attention until the 1990s when generative artists started to collaborate with mathematicians and scientists, resulting in a more complex and sophisticated form of generative art.

This collaboration between artists and scientists led to the creation of complex computer codes that could generate visual images based on mathematical formulas. This development brought a new level of complexity to generative art since it was no longer just about generating simple lines or shapes; now it involved intricate algorithms that could create complex designs. One example of this is fractal art, which uses mathematical formulas to create self-similar patterns that repeat infinitely. It is mesmerizing how these patterns create intricate designs that are both beautiful and mathematically precise.

Another example is algorithmic art, which uses mathematical algorithms to produce works of art. The challenge for these artists is not just creating an algorithm but also determining how much control they want over the final outcome. Some may choose to have complete control over every aspect, while others may allow some randomness in the process. One example of Midjourney's capabilities is an image generated from the prompt "**a red bird sitting on a branch**." The resulting image shows a beautifully detailed bird perched on a branch against a blue sky background. The level of detail is astounding, with even the individual feathers on the bird's wings clearly visible.

DALL-E

DALL-E is another text-to-image generation system that was developed by OpenAI. This neural network model can generate images from textual descriptions, allowing it to create stunning artwork based on mere words. Launched in January 2021, DALL-E has already made waves in the art world for its ability to combine human creativity with machine learning algorithms. DALL-E's name is derived from the iconic Pixar character WALL-E and artist Salvador Dalí. Like these two inspirations, DALL-E is a masterpiece of art and science that pushes the boundaries of what we know about creativity and artificial intelligence. The system was trained on millions of images, allowing it to recognize patterns and generate original artworks based on specific textual prompts.

It can generate high-quality images from textual descriptions that are far more complex than those used by Midjourney. For example, DALL-E can create an image based on prompts such as "**an armchair in the shape of an avocado**" or "**a snail made out of harp strings**." One particularly impressive example created using DALL-E is an image generated from the prompt "an illustration of a baby daikon radish in a tutu walking her dog." The resulting image shows just that – a baby daikon radish wearing a tutu and walking a dog. The level of detail in the image is incredible, with even the folds of the tutu and the individual leaves on the dog's collar clearly visible.

DALL-E has created some truly remarkable pieces that have caught the attention of artists and enthusiasts alike. One such artwork features an armchair shaped like an avocado, while another depicts a snail made entirely out of harpsichords. These surreal creations demonstrate the power of DALL-E's algorithmic creativity, which can produce art that is both whimsical and thought-provoking. While some skeptics may argue that DALL-E isn't truly "creating" art since it relies on pre-existing data sets, others argue that this technology represents a new form of collaboration between human imagination and machine learning algorithms. Regardless of how one chooses to view it, there's no denying that DALL-E is an impressive feat of engineering that has breathed new life into the concept of generative AI art.

The GeniusBehind DALL-E: Meet GPT-3

DALL-E, the revolutionary AI artist that has taken the art world by storm, owes its creative power to GPT-3. Short for Generative

Pre-trained Transformer 3, it is a state-of-the-art language model developed by OpenAI that has been trained on an enormous corpus of text data. This impressive neural network has revolutionized the way we interact with technology and paved the way for new frontiers in artificial intelligence. GPT-3 is a generative language model that can produce human-like text output based on a given prompt. It relies on machine learning algorithms to predict what comes next in a sentence or paragraph and generate corresponding responses. With its ability to understand context and syntax, GPT-3 is capable of creating coherent and insightful written content that resembles something truly human.

This remarkable innovation was created with the goal of enabling machines to perform tasks traditionally requiring human intelligence such as writing essays, composing poetry, or even creating artwork like DALL-E's stunning images. Its ability to generate text from scratch means it can create unique descriptions of people, places, things, and ideas that have never existed before. Not only does GPT-3 have practical applications in generating useful content like chatbot responses or automatic summarization of news articles but also has creative uses such as developing scripts for movies and games or helping writers overcome writer's block by suggesting ideas for their work. It presents an unprecedented opportunity for people to engage with technology in new ways and even break down barriers between humans and machines.

Diffusion

Diffusion is a recent addition to the world of text prompt generative art. It uses an algorithm called diffusion models to generate images from textual descriptions, with a particular focus on creating abstract or surreal images. One example created using Diffusion is an image based on the prompt "**a sunset over a city made of glass**." The resulting image shows an abstract cityscape made up of swirling colors and shapes against a sunset background.

Leonardo.ai

Finally, **Leonardo.ai** is another exciting development in this field. It uses natural language processing and machine learning algorithms to generate artwork based on textual prompts. One example created using Leonardo.ai is an image generated from the prompt "a woman walking through a misty forest." The resulting image shows a beautifully detailed forest scene, with mist swirling around the trees and a woman walking through it. Advancements in AI art technology are transforming the way we create and consume art. As machines become better at creating content that rivals human creativity, it's important for us to embrace these changes while also being aware of their potential implications. By working together - artists and technologists alike - we can push boundaries and create an entirely new era of artistic expression that was once unimaginable.

Other Types

Generative art and style transfer are just two examples of how AI can be used in creative expression. Other forms include:

- **Interactive installations:** Combining AI with sensors or other input devices to create immersive experiences that respond to viewer actions or environmental cues.

- **Data visualization:** Using AI algorithms to transform complex datasets into compelling visualizations that help people better understand and interpret data.

- **Musical composition:** Using AI algorithms to generate new musical compositions that incorporate elements from existing works or other sources. AI can also be used for interactive installations, data visualization, and musical composition by combining it with sensors or input devices, transforming complex datasets, or generating new compositions incorporating elements from existing works.

The possibilities are virtually endless when it comes to AI art. As machine learning technologies continue to evolve, we can expect even more innovative and boundary-pushing works from artists who dare to explore this exciting new frontier of creativity.

IMPACT AND POSSIBILITIES

The Impact of AI on the Artistic Process

The world of art has been revolutionized by advancements in artificial intelligence (AI) technology. With access to new techniques and tools, artists can now create works that were once unimaginable. One of the most significant impacts of AI technology on the artistic process is the ability for artists to work faster and more efficiently. With software like Adobe Photoshop or Illustrator, artists can quickly sketch out ideas and make changes without worrying about damaging their original work. This allows them to experiment with new techniques and styles without fear of failure.

Another benefit is that AI technology can provide artists with endless inspiration. For instance, Google's Deep Dream algorithm allows artists to input an image and have it transformed into a surrealistic dream-like vision by using neural networks. The possibilities are limitless, from creating abstract shapes to realistic landscapes. Furthermore, AI technology offers an opportunity for collaboration between humans and machines. Artists can use applications like Artbreeder or

RunwayML to generate unique images that they wouldn't be able to produce on their own. These programs use machine learning algorithms that analyze large sets of data and generate new visuals based on specific parameters set by the artist.

However, while there are numerous benefits associated with using AI in art, there are also potential ethical concerns surrounding its use in creating original works of art. For example, some argue that using AI-generated images could diminish creativity since machines are generating ideas instead of humans. Despite these concerns, it is clear that advancements in AI-based technologies have had a profound impact on the artistic process. From faster workflows to endless inspiration sources and collaboration opportunities with machines; these technologies offer a plethora of benefits for contemporary artists.

Exploring AI's Possibilities in Art

The world of art is changing, and rapidly so. The advancements in AI technology have opened up new possibilities for artists to express themselves in ways that were previously impossible. From generating complex images to creating entire pieces of music, AI has the potential to change the way we think about creativity. But what exactly are these possibilities? How are they being used today, and what might they look like in the future? In this chapter, I'll explore some of these questions and attempt to provide a glimpse into the exciting world of AI-generated art.

One of the most obvious uses for AI in art is as a tool for generating images. This can be seen in everything from simple digital illustrations to complex 3D models. One example of this is the use of "style transfer," which involves taking an existing image and applying a different artistic style to it. Another use for AI in art is as a tool for creating music. This might seem like an odd concept at first, but it's actually quite natural when you consider how music is often created today. Many composers already use computer programs to help them write music, so introducing AI into this process isn't much of a stretch.

Of course, there are also ethical implications surrounding the use of AI-generated art. For one thing, there's the question of whether or not such art can truly be considered "art" at all. Some argue that because it's created by machines rather than humans, it lacks the emotional depth and complexity that we usually associate with creative works. There's also concern over who owns these creations once they're made. If an artist uses an algorithm created by someone else to generate their work, who does that work belong to? Should it be considered intellectual property?

Despite these concerns, however, there's no denying that AI has opened up exciting new avenues for artistic expression. As technology continues to advance, we can only expect to see more and more artists experimenting with these tools in order to create truly unique and innovative works. It's impossible to predict exactly what the future of AI-generated art will look like, but one thing is clear: it's going to be exciting. Whether it's through the development of new techniques or the use of increasingly sophisticated algorithms, there's no limit to what we might be able to achieve with this technology.

As AI technology continues to evolve, we can expect to see more sophisticated and advanced AI artists emerge. These artists will have greater capabilities to interpret text prompts and generate increasingly complex and intricate artwork. This development could lead to new forms of artistic expression that would be impossible for human artists to create. Imagine entire galleries filled with breathtaking generative art pieces that push boundaries never before considered possible! In addition to becoming more advanced and sophisticated, generative AI art is expected to become more integrated with other technologies such as virtual reality (VR) and augmented reality (AR). This integration could create entirely new ways for people to experience art. Imagine being transported into a virtual gallery where you can interact with generative artworks like never before. Or imagine walking through an augmented reality exhibit where the artwork comes alive all around you. The possibilities are truly endless!

Chapter Three

Applications of Artificial Intelligence Across Different Forms of Art

Photography

Artificial Intelligence has the potential to revolutionize not only the way we produce art but also how we consume it. From photography to literature, AI can be used as an aid towards creativity in a variety of forms of art, making the process faster, more efficient, and even more imaginative. One area where AI is already making waves is in **photography**. With computer vision algorithms and deep learning techniques, AI can analyze images and generate new ones that are realistic and visually striking. For example, let's say you are a photographer who wants to create a composite image by combining multiple shots into one seamless panorama. Instead of manually stitching the images together, you can use an AI-powered tool like Hugin or Autostitch to do the job for you.

Through the utilization of computer vision algorithms and deep learning techniques, AI can analyze images and generate new ones that possess a striking visual appeal and a sense of realism. Consider a scenario where a photographer seeks to create a panoramic composite image by seamlessly merging multiple shots. Instead of laboriously stitching the images together manually, AI-powered tools such as Hugin or Autostitch can swiftly accomplish the task, freeing up the artist's time and energy for other creative pursuits.

Music

Music composition is another domain that has undergone a profound transformation through the intervention of AI. By employing machine learning algorithms capable of recognizing patterns within vast musical data sets, AI can assist composers in generating novel melodies and harmonies that may have eluded them otherwise. This technology has already found applications in the realm of custom music creation for television shows and commercials, with companies like **Amper Music** leveraging AI to compose music that resonates with specific narratives and emotions; and to create custom-made music for TV shows and commercials.

Art

Artificial Intelligence (AI) has emerged as a transformative force in the **world of art**, revolutionizing both the production and consumption of artistic creations. From photography to literature, AI has the power to enhance creativity across various art forms, enabling artists to streamline their processes, achieve greater efficiency, and explore uncharted realms of imagination.

Literature

The influence of AI extends even to the realm of literature. Recently, **OpenAI** introduced an algorithm capable of producing coherent news articles based on written prompts. While this technology is yet to be widely embraced by authors and publishers, it presents an exciting glimpse into the potential future of AI-assisted literary endeavors. However, the integration of AI into different art forms raises ethical considerations. One significant concern revolves around the notion of authenticity and artificiality. When an AI algorithm generates a piece of music or literature, questions arise regarding the attribution of authorship and the status of such creations as genuine art. These dilemmas highlight the complex interplay between human creativity and the involvement of artificial intelligence.

Notwithstanding these concerns, the integration of AI tools into artistic workflows offers boundless opportunities for artists to push the boundaries of their own creativity. It is ultimately the prerogative of each artist to determine how and when they incorporate AI into their creative processes. Nonetheless, one fact remains clear: the incorporation of AI has the potential to unleash unparalleled creative potential across various art forms. Crucially, it is vital to recognize that AI does not seek to replace human creativity; rather, it acts as a tool that amplifies our imaginations and expands the horizons of artistic expression. By embracing AI technologies within the context of different art forms, artists can continue to redefine the limits of their craft and produce groundbreaking work that inspires future generations.

The integration of AI across various art forms holds tremendous promise for artists seeking to push the boundaries of their creativity. From photography to music composition and literature, AI tools offer unprecedented opportunities to enhance artistic processes and explore new realms of imaginative expression. While ethical questions persist, artists can navigate these complexities by recognizing AI as a collaborative tool, one that empowers them to delve deeper into their craft and create awe-inspiring works that captivate audiences worldwide. Embracing AI in the artistic process enables artists to embark on a journey of boundless innovation, unshackled by limitations, and forever reshaping the landscape of art itself.

Chapter Four

Embracing AI in the Artistic Process

The fusion of artificial intelligence (AI) and artistic expression presents a realm of endless possibilities, necessitating a deep understanding of AI's role in this revolutionary paradigm. The integration of AI tools has paved the way for revolutionary creative opportunities, transcending the boundaries of our imaginations. At its core, this artistic revolution revolves around embracing new technologies such as AI as aides rather than replacements for human creativity. It emphasizes enhancing our existing abilities rather than succumbing to the dominance of machines. By collaborating with AI tools, artists can navigate uncharted territories, pushing boundaries beyond their wildest dreams.

The true beauty of this artistic revolution lies in the symbiotic relationship between humans and machines. Artists contribute their unique perspectives and creative visions, while AI technology aids in tasks such as image manipulation and music composition. Together, they create remarkable works that would have been inconceivable without the mutual influence. A prime example of this collaboration is seen in generative art, where algorithms generate unique pieces based on artistic input. Although these works surpass what human hands alone can create, they still retain authenticity thanks to the artist's influence on the creative process.

However, amidst these exciting advancements, challenges must be addressed as we forge ahead. One primary challenge involves ensuring that artists do not become excessively reliant on AI tools at the expense of their own creativity. It is vital to remember that while AI can assist, it cannot replace human intuition or imagination. Additionally, ethical considerations surrounding the use of AI in art creation demand attention. Navigating the fine line between authenticity and artificiality necessitates careful deliberation and thoughtfulness when leveraging these powerful tools.

Despite these challenges, countless opportunities for growth within this field emerge as more artists embrace new technologies like AI. By maintaining an open mind toward innovation and expanding our creative horizons, we can continuously push the boundaries of artistic expression. The ongoing artistic revolution serves as a testament to human ingenuity and creativity. By embracing AI as a means to unlock new creative opportunities and explore uncharted territories, we tap into its potential. It is crucial to remember that AI serves as an aid rather than a replacement for human creativity. Collaborating with these tools enables us to achieve extraordinary feats in the realm of art.

As we stand at the forefront of the fourth industrial revolution, artists naturally gravitate toward embracing technologies that can aid their creative processes. Among these technologies, Artificial Intelligence (AI) has made significant waves in the art world. With its capacity to learn and analyze vast amounts of data, AI tools have seamlessly integrated into the workflows of many artists. However, before delving into the realm of AI-assisted art, artists must comprehend which tools best suit their unique needs. The market offers a variety of AI tools, each with its own strengths and weaknesses. Some tools excel in generating ideas, while others specialize in image recognition or style transfer.

In the ever-evolving art world, the integration of artificial intelligence (AI) emerges as a potent tool, offering artists the potential to unlock new realms of creativity. After artists carefully select the appropriate AI tool, the next step involves seamlessly incorporating it into their creative workflow. This entails identifying the areas where AI can provide the most assistance and utilizing these tools as aids rather than replacements. By effectively harnessing the capabilities of AI, artists embark on a transformative journey that expands their artistic horizons.

Consider a painter who decides to incorporate style transfer algorithms into their artistic process. These algorithms prove invaluable, enabling the artist to generate unique textures and captivating color palettes they may not have conceived on their own. With a simple application of AI, the artist can explore an extensive range of artistic styles, experiment with innovative approaches, and infuse their artwork with fresh energy. Integrating AI becomes akin to collaborating with a virtual partner, guiding the artist toward unexplored avenues of artistic expression.

Another compelling aspect of embracing AI lies in the realm of image recognition algorithms. Artists dealing with complex datasets can leverage these algorithms to uncover patterns and gain deeper insights into their subject matter. By harnessing the analytical power of AI, artists can extract meaningful information from extensive visual data, unearthing hidden connections and inspiring visual motifs. The integration of AI-driven image recognition expands the artist's creative toolkit, enabling them to communicate their message more effectively.

Nevertheless, amidst the undeniable benefits that accompany the use of AI-assisted art creation methods, ethical considerations must be carefully addressed. When creating art with AI, questions of authenticity and originality can arise, particularly when utilizing generative models that produce artwork without direct human input. It is essential for artists to approach these considerations thoughtfully, ensuring that the integrity of their artistic vision remains intact. AI should be viewed as a tool that amplifies creativity rather than replacing the artist's unique perspective.

It is crucial to recognize that while AI can assist in generating ideas and identifying patterns within datasets, it cannot fully replicate human creativity. Each artist possesses a distinct blend of emotions, experiences, and personal viewpoints that breathe life into their work. It is the human touch that imbues art with a profound sense of individuality and resonates with viewers on a deeply emotional level. Thus, artists must strike a delicate balance between leveraging AI tools to enhance their creative process and infusing their work with the essence of their own humanity.

Embracing AI in the artistic process opens the door to new creative opportunities and has the potential to revolutionize the art world as we know it. However, artists must approach the integration of AI tools into their workflows thoughtfully and ethically. By experimenting with various AI technologies and utilizing them as aids rather than replacements, artists can unleash their creativity in ways that transcend imagination. The key lies in striking a harmonious balance between AI-driven assistance and the artist's unique perspective. AI should be viewed as a catalyst, expanding the artist's potential and encouraging exploration. By embracing the possibilities that AI offers, artists can redefine the limits of their artistic expression, exploring uncharted territories and challenging conventions.

To truly harness the transformative power of AI, artists must embrace a mindset of continuous experimentation. Exploring different AI technologies and their applications can lead to groundbreaking discoveries and novel approaches to artistic creation. It is through this exploration that artists can unearth new dimensions of their creativity, leading to breakthroughs that captivate and inspire. However, in this journey, artists must never lose sight of the ethical implications of integrating AI into their artistic process. They must always remain mindful of preserving their artistic integrity, ensuring that AI remains a tool that enhances their creativity rather than overshadowing it.

So, the fusion of AI and artistic expression represents a realm of limitless possibilities. By embracing AI as a collaborative tool, artists can unlock new avenues of creativity and explore uncharted territories. The integration of AI offers new ways to generate ideas, manipulate images, and enhance artistic styles. However, artists must approach AI thoughtfully and ethically, striking a balance between utilizing AI tools and preserving their unique artistic perspective. AI should be viewed as an aid rather than a replacement for human creativity, amplifying the artist's potential while maintaining the authenticity and emotional depth that comes from human involvement. By embracing AI with an open mind, artists can push the boundaries of artistic expression, revolutionizing the art world and creating remarkable works that captivate and inspire audiences.

Chapter Five

Ethical Considerations in AI Art

The Challenge of Ethical Considerations

While integrating AI into your artistic workflow can provide significant benefits, there are ethical considerations you need to be aware of. Many artists are exploring the ethical implications of using AI in their work, such as ownership rights or the legitimacy of AI-generated art. It's crucial for artists to stay informed about these issues as they integrate AI into their creative processes. Understanding these considerations is essential for maintaining artistic integrity while embracing the potential benefits of using technology in art creation.

Understanding the ethical implications of AI-generated art

As AI art becomes more prevalent, it is important to consider the ethical implications of using artificial intelligence to create art. While AI-generated art can be stunning and innovative, it also raises questions about authorship, ownership, and authenticity. Moreover, as we entrust more decisions to algorithms, we need to ensure that the outcome aligns with our moral values. One major concern is that AI could automate human creativity and replace human artists. This fear stems from a misunderstanding of how AI works. AI is not creative in the same way humans are; it can only generate new artworks based on existing data. Therefore, while AI may augment or assist human creativity, it cannot completely replace it. Another ethical issue is discrimination in training data. If an algorithm is trained on biased or incomplete data sets, its output may perpetuate existing inequalities and stereotypes. For example, a facial recognition algorithm that was trained disproportionately on white faces may misidentify people with darker skin tones as criminals or terrorists.

To address these issues, artists must be transparent about their use of AI tools and disclose any data sets they used for training their models. They should also advocate for diversity in data selection to prevent discrimination or bias in their output. One of the primary concerns surrounding AI-generated art is whether or not it can be considered truly authentic. Some argue that since AI algorithms are programmed by humans, any artwork created with them is essentially a derivative work. Others argue that because the algorithms are capable of generating entirely new compositions and styles, they should be recognized as original works in their own right.

When using Neural Networks and AI Art Generators, we must consider the ethical implications. These technologies are groundbreaking, but they come with complex ethical considerations that demand serious attention. One significant concern is copyright infringement. It is crucial to **avoid using other artists' work to train**

our networks or create new art. Such actions are not only unethical but also illegal, and they could result in legal consequences.

To prevent these problems, it is advisable to only **use images that are your art, belong to you, or for which you possess copyright permission**. This may require extra effort, but it is essential for staying within the boundaries of the law and preserving your integrity as an artist. Another ethical issue involves the use of AI-generated art created by others for commercial purposes. Although there may be no legal barriers, some argue that profiting from someone else's creation in this manner raises moral questions. However, this topic is complex, and different perspectives exist. Some believe that AI-generated art can inspire artists with new ideas and techniques, while others argue that it diminishes the value of original artistic expression and undermines creativity. Ultimately, each artist must decide their comfort level in using AI-generated art for commercial purposes. Nevertheless, it is vital to carefully consider the impact of your actions on other artists in this field.

Despite these challenges, there are steps that artists can take to ensure they are using AI ethically in their creative process. One approach is to be transparent about how they are using these tools and give credit where credit is due – both to themselves as well as any collaborators or programming sources involved in creating an artwork. Another important consideration is ensuring that data used by these algorithms come from diverse sources so that bias can be minimized as much as possible. Artists must also educate themselves on the laws and regulations surrounding AI-generated art to ensure they are not inadvertently infringing on someone else's intellectual property.

In the end, it is important to remember that AI is a tool, not a replacement for human creativity. While it offers exciting new possibilities for artistic expression, it is ultimately up to the artist to decide how they want to integrate this technology into their workflow. With careful consideration and ethical practices, AI-generated art can be a powerful force for positive change in the art world.

Chapter Six

Opportunities and Challenges with AI in Art

Artists have always been at the forefront of innovation, pushing boundaries and exploring new mediums. The integration of artificial intelligence (AI) into the artistic process is no exception. However, as with any emerging technology, there are both challenges and opportunities that come along with it. One of the main challenges of using AI in art is navigating the fine line between authenticity and artificiality. While AI can assist artists in creating unique works, there is a fear that it may lead to a loss of human creativity and originality. It is important for artists to understand that AI should serve as an aid rather than a replacement for their own creative process. Another challenge is ensuring that AI-generated art meets ethical standards. There are concerns about ownership rights, accountability for mistakes made by algorithms, and potential biases within the technology itself. Artists must be aware of these issues when using AI tools and take steps to ensure they are creating ethical works.

Despite these challenges, there are many opportunities for innovation and growth within the field. For example, AI can help artists create more complex works by analyzing large amounts of data or identifying patterns that humans may not see on their own. It can also assist with tasks such as color selection or composition layout. Moreover, AI can open up new forms of artistic expression that were previously unimaginable. For instance, machine learning algorithms can analyze existing artworks to create entirely new pieces based on certain styles or themes. This has led to exciting collaborations between artists and programmers where they work together to create something truly unique.

Lastly, advancements in technology have made using AI tools more accessible than ever before. Many software companies now offer user-friendly platforms specifically designed for artists looking to integrate machine learning into their workflow. As we continue down this path towards an Artistic Revolution fueled by artificial intelligence it's important not only embrace these technological advances but also recognize its limitations while still being able to harness its power. Ultimately the role of AI in art should be viewed as an aid to complement human creativity, not replace it entirely.

DIFFERENT PURPOSES FOR AI ART

The field of AI-generated art has opened up a whole new world of creative possibilities. From generating unique images for advertisements, to using AI-generated art in film and media, the potential uses are endless. Here are some different ways AI-generated art can be used:

Commercial Uses

The advertising industry is always looking for new and innovative ways to create eye-catching ads that grab viewers' attention. AI-generated art can be used to create unique images that stand out from the crowd. By analyzing data on consumer preferences and trends, AI algorithms can generate images that are specifically tailored to appeal to a particular target audience. Another commercial use of AI-generated art is in product design. With the help of machine learning algorithms, designers can create 3D models of products quickly and easily, without having to spend hours creating them manually.

Creative Uses

AI-generated art is also finding its way into the world of fine arts. Several artists have experimented with using machine learning algorithms to create unique pieces of art that would be impossible for humans to produce on their own. In addition, filmmakers are using AI algorithms to generate special effects for movies and TV shows. The technology can also be used to create entire virtual worlds or landscapes that would be too difficult or expensive to build in real life.

Educational Uses

AI-generated art can also be used as a teaching tool in educational settings. For example, it can help students learn about different styles of artwork by generating examples from various eras and regions around the world. In addition, machine learning algorithms can analyze large amounts of data on famous artists and their works and generate insights about their techniques and styles. This could help students learn more about the history of art and how it has evolved over time.

Therapeutic Uses

Sometimes, simply creating art can be therapeutic for people dealing with mental health issues. AI-generated art can provide a safe and accessible outlet for those struggling with anxiety, depression, or other mental health challenges. AI-generated art can also be used in art therapy programs to help patients express themselves creatively and explore their emotions through different mediums. As machine learning algorithms become more advanced, the possibilities for using AI-generated art as a therapeutic tool will only continue to grow.

While it's important for artists to be aware of the challenges and ethical considerations that come with using AI in their work, the opportunities for innovation and growth within the field are immense. When used correctly, AI can assist artists in creating truly unique works that push the boundaries of traditional artistic expression. The future of art lies in embracing these new technologies and finding ways to collaborate with them to unleash creativity beyond our imagination.

Chapter Seven

Integrating AI into your Artistic Workflow

The world of art has always been about pushing boundaries and exploring new ways of expressing oneself. Over the years, traditional techniques have been refined and perfected, resulting in some truly stunning works of art. However, with the advent of AI tools and technology, artists now have even more possibilities to explore. The concept of combining traditional techniques with AI tools is not new. In fact, it has been around for quite some time. But what exactly does this mean? Simply put, it means using algorithms and machine learning to enhance or augment traditional art techniques.

For instance, an artist could use a deep learning algorithm to generate unique color palettes that they can then incorporate into their paintings or drawings. Alternatively, an artist could use AI tools to create complex patterns or textures that would be difficult if not impossible to create by hand. By combining these two distinct approaches to art-making, artists can push the boundaries of creativity even further than before. They can experiment with new styles and approaches while still retaining the essence of traditional techniques.

One major advantage of using AI tools in this way is that it expands creative possibilities exponentially. Artists are no longer limited by what they can do by hand alone; instead, they have access to a whole range of digital tools that can help them achieve their vision more efficiently and effectively. Of course, this doesn't mean that traditional techniques are any less important than they were before. In fact, quite the opposite is true - mastering traditional techniques provides a solid foundation upon which artists can build their AI-enhanced creations.

In this chapter we will explore these concepts in greater depth: we will look at how traditional techniques can be used as a starting point for incorporating AI tools, examine some specific advantages that these digital tools bring, see how AI-generated artwork can inspire new ideas, and encourage artists to break free from rules when combining these two approaches. But for now, let us simply marvel at the possibilities that arise when we combine traditional techniques with AI tools. The sky truly is the limit when it comes to art-making, and this is just the beginning.

The Importance of Traditional Techniques

Art is a form of expression that has been around for centuries, and throughout time, traditional techniques have played a crucial role in shaping the art world. From painting to sculpture, these techniques have provided artists with a foundation to build upon and create works of art that are both beautiful and impactful. The importance of traditional techniques cannot be overstated. They provide a sense of history and tradition that connects artists with their predecessors. It's through these techniques that we've seen the evolution of art over the years, from the Renaissance period to modern times. One significant advantage of traditional techniques is the level of control they provide an artist. When using them, an artist can manipulate every aspect of their work, from texture to color, shape, and form. Additionally, these techniques allow for greater precision when creating art pieces.

Another reason why traditional techniques are important is because they allow an artist to develop their skills over time. With practice comes mastery; as artists continue to work on honing their craft using these methods, they can develop new styles and approaches that set them apart from others. Incorporating AI tools into art doesn't mean abandoning traditional methods altogether; instead, it means expanding creative possibilities by combining both old and new ways of creating art. By doing so, artists can create pieces that are more complex and layered than ever before.

When using AI tools in combination with traditional methods like drawing or painting, they can add depth to artwork by providing unique textures or patterns not readily available through manual creation alone. These digital tools also enable artists to experiment with different color palettes or visual effects quickly without having to start from scratch each time they want to make changes. Furthermore, incorporating AI-generated elements into artwork has allowed for some truly groundbreaking works in recent years. For example, some contemporary artists have used machine learning algorithms to train computers how humans perceive beauty or identify specific objects like faces or landscapes. These computer-generated images then serve as references and inspiration for artists, allowing them to create unique pieces that are both visually stunning and thought-provoking.

The Advantages of AI Tools

As technologies continue to evolve, the art world has not been left behind. One of the most recent technologies that have been introduced in the field of art is AI tools. These tools have revolutionized the way artists approach their work. They provide a new level of depth and complexity that traditional techniques alone cannot achieve. In this chapter, we will explore some of the advantages of using AI tools in art. AI tools offer a wide range of benefits that can enhance an artist's creative process. For example, they can help increase productivity by automating repetitive tasks such as color correction and image enhancement. This allows artists to focus on more critical aspects of their work, such as composition and storytelling. Moreover, AI tools can be used to generate new ideas and inspiration for artists who are struggling with creative blocks. These tools can analyze vast amounts of data and produce unique designs that an artist may not have thought about before.

Another advantage is that AI-generated content can be used as a starting point for further exploration through traditional techniques. Artists can use these generated designs as references or inspiration when creating their own works using traditional methods such as painting or drawing. It is also worth noting that AI-generated content provides an opportunity for artists to experiment with new styles and techniques without committing too much time or resources to them upfront. This flexibility allows artists to take risks without fear of failure since they know they can always go back and make changes later. However, it's important to remember that while AI tools do offer many benefits, they should never replace traditional techniques entirely. Traditional techniques provide a solid foundation upon which artists build their skills over time; hence they remain essential in learning different aspects such as composition, color theory, form anatomy among others.

The Reverse Workflow – AI Art as a Reference

As artists, we have always found inspiration in the world around us. Whether it be nature, architecture, or even other artists' works, every piece of art has its roots in something tangible. With the advent of AI tools and technology, a new source of inspiration has become available to us. We can now generate art that is purely digital and has never before existed. However, as we explore the possibilities of AI-generated art, it's important not to forget our traditional techniques. In this section, we'll explore how to use AI-generated art as references and inspiration to create new pieces using traditional methods. We call this approach the reverse workflow. Traditionally when creating a piece of artwork, an artist would begin with a physical reference point such as a photograph or sketch. They would then use their skills and creativity to translate that reference into their own unique vision. However, with AI-generated art as our reference point, we can take things one step further. By combining the best aspects of both traditional techniques and AI tools, we can create works that are more complex and nuanced than ever before.

One way to start is by using an AI tool such as StyleGAN2-ADA to generate a variety of images based on different styles or themes. These generated images can serve as references for artists looking for new ideas or fresh perspectives on old themes. Once an artist finds an image they like from the generated set, they can take it into their preferred medium such as painting or sculpture and begin working on their interpretation. This allows them to incorporate their own unique style while still benefiting from the added depth and complexity provided by the AI-generated reference material.

However, it's important not to rely too heavily on these generated images. While they can be incredibly useful sources of inspiration in your creative process; ultimately your work should reflect your own vision rather than just being a copy-and-paste job from an AI-generated image. The reverse workflow of AI art as a reference or catalyst for traditional methods, allows us to expand our creative possibilities while still staying rooted in traditional techniques. By combining the best aspects of both worlds, we can create works that are truly unique and groundbreaking.

Breaking the Rules (The Ones That Can be Broken)

When it comes to combining traditional techniques with AI tools, there are no hard and fast rules. The beauty of this approach lies in the freedom to be authentic and innovative without being bound by any restrictions or conventions. Artists who embrace this approach understand that while traditional techniques provide a foundation for their work, they can reach new heights of creativity by incorporating AI tools. However, it is important not to let these tools take over and instead use them as a means of enhancing their artistic vision.

To truly break the rules, artists must first understand what they are. Traditionally, art was created through specific mediums such as paint on canvas or charcoal on paper. However, with the advent of AI tools, artists can now create digital art that is just as valid. One way to embrace this new form of creation is through experimentation.

By using AI-generated art as references or inspiration for further exploration with traditional methods, artists can push boundaries and create something truly unique. Another way to break the rules is by incorporating unexpected elements into your work. Whether it's a bold color choice or an unconventional subject matter, taking risks can lead to exciting discoveries and innovations in your artwork.

It's also important not to become too attached to one particular style or technique when combining traditional methods with AI tools. Instead, allow yourself room for growth and change as you continue exploring this new approach. Finally, don't be afraid to seek out feedback from others who have experience working with both traditional techniques and AI tools. Collaborating with other artists can help you expand your knowledge base while also providing valuable insights into how different mediums interact with each other. AI is revolutionizing the creative industry, and it is essential to integrate it into your artistic workflow. You need to understand how AI-generated art can help you create more complex and engaging artwork. In this section, we will explore the benefits of integrating AI into your artistic workflow.

Enhanced Creativity and Efficiency

One of the most significant benefits of integrating AI into your artistic workflow is enhanced creativity and efficiency. AI algorithms can analyze massive amounts of data, identify patterns, and make suggestions that can inspire new creative ideas. By using an AI tool to generate a base image or design concept, artists have been able to develop more complex pieces of art in less time. Incorporating AI tools into the early stages of a project allows artists to focus more on creative decision-making rather than technical execution. This approach can save time and energy while enhancing the overall quality of the final piece.

Collaboration with Machines

The integration of AI tools into an artist's toolkit enables collaboration with machines that offer new perspectives on creating art. Instead of seeing these tools as replacements for human creativity, artists who have embraced them view these algorithms as collaborators that enhance their own creative processes. This collaboration between humans and machines has led to groundbreaking art that pushes boundaries previously unexplored by either party alone. With this collaboration, artists are not limited by their own experience or skills but have the ability to use technology as a tool for exploration in their work.

New Techniques and Styles

Another benefit of integrating AI tools into an artist's workflow is discovering new techniques and styles that would be challenging or impossible without these tools' help. With access to advanced deep learning algorithms, artists can create entirely new styles and techniques that were previously impossible to imagine. For example, some artists have used AI algorithms to blend different styles of artwork, creating entirely new art forms that have never existed before. These new techniques and styles allow artists to push the limits of creativity and create work that is both unique and groundbreaking.

The Art of Selecting the Right AI Tools

Artificial Intelligence (AI) has revolutionized the way artists create, allowing them to access a whole new world of possibilities. With so many options available, it can be challenging to find the right tools that fit your artistic style and vision. It is important to keep in mind that no tool is perfect, and it is up to you to decide which ones will help you achieve your creative goals.

Understanding AI Art Tools

The first step in selecting the best AI art tools for your work is understanding what they can do. Most AI art tools use deep learning algorithms, which enable them to recognize patterns and make predictions based on data input. These tools can generate a wide range of styles, from realistic images to abstract compositions. It's crucial to understand the capabilities of each tool so you can choose one that aligns with your vision.

Choosing a Tool That Complements Your Style

There are many different types of AI art tools available, each with its own strengths and weaknesses. Some tools may be better suited for artists who prefer more abstract compositions, while others may be ideal for those who prefer more realistic images. It's essential to experiment with various tools until you find one that complements your style the best.

Taking Into Account Ease of Use and Accessibility

In addition to finding an AI tool that fits your artistic style, you also need one that is easy to use and accessible. Some programs require a steep learning curve; others have intuitive interfaces designed for artists without programming experience. Additionally, consider how accessible these platforms are – some apps or software may cost quite a bit or even offer pay-to-use subscriptions while others are free but have limited features.

Maintaining Ethical Considerations

AI art has quickly become a topic of ethical discussion within the artistic community. When selecting AI tools, it's essential to keep in mind how the algorithms were created and whether their output is ethical. Some tools may have been trained using biased data or produce results that are not desired. As an artist, it is your responsibility to ensure that you are producing ethical and socially responsible work. Choosing the right AI tool for your needs requires careful consideration of several factors, including your artistic style, ease of use, and accessibility. It's essential to experiment with various programs until you find one that complements your artistic vision while still producing ethically sound work. With these considerations in mind, you can unleash your creativity with AI art and push the boundaries of what is possible in the world of art.

How to unleash your creativity with AI art

AI art is a revolutionary tool that allows artists to break free from traditional constraints and explore new horizons of creativity. But how can you use AI art to unleash your creative potential? Here are some tips:

1. Experiment with different AI tools

The first step to unleashing your creativity with AI art is to experiment with different AI tools. Each tool has its unique features, strengths, and limitations. Try out several tools and see which ones work best for you. Don't be afraid to mix and match different tools and techniques to create something truly unique.

2. Embrace randomness

One of the most exciting aspects of using AI in art is the element of randomness that it brings into the creative process. Don't be afraid to let go of control and let the algorithms generate unexpected results. Sometimes, embracing randomness can lead you down an entirely new artistic path that you never would have imagined otherwise.

3. Find inspiration in existing artworks

A great way to get started with AI-generated art is by finding inspiration in existing artworks. You can feed an image into an algorithm and see what sort of variations it generates, or even use an existing artwork as a starting point for your own creation.

4. Collaborate with other artists

Last but not least, collaborating with other artists is a fantastic way to unleash your creativity with AI-generated art. Working with others can not only give you new perspectives on your own work but also allow you to explore new ideas and techniques. Using AI technology in art allows us as creatives more freedom than ever before when it comes time for us to create our next masterpiece. When using such technology one is able to experiment with different tools, embrace randomness, find inspiration in existing artworks and collaborate with other artists.

Chapter Eight

Tips and Tricks for Creating Stunning AI-Generated Art

Creating art is one of the most significant human achievements that reflect our creativity and imagination. However, creating art is not an easy task. It requires originality, innovation, and a lot of practice. But what if we tell you that you can create stunning pieces of art with the help of AI? Yes, that's right! With the recent advancements in artificial intelligence (AI), it has become possible to generate stunning and unique pieces of art without any human intervention. In this chapter, we will discuss some tips and tricks to create stunning AI-generated art.

Use of Text Prompts for AI-Generated Art

One of the most fascinating features of AI-generated art is its ability to create something unique and unpredictable in response to a text prompt. In other words, you can give an AI model a few words or a sentence, and it will generate an image based on the text. This feature has opened up new avenues for creating art that are truly one-of-a-kind. The use of text prompts for creating AI-generated art has become increasingly popular in recent years. The reason is simple: it allows artists to express their creativity without having to worry too much about technical details. Just by providing a few words or sentences, artists can get interesting results that they can then refine and tweak until they are happy with the final product.

To make the most out of text prompts for AI-generated art, it's important to understand how they work. Basically, when you provide a text prompt, the AI model uses natural language processing (NLP) techniques to analyze and understand the meaning behind the words. It then generates an image based on that understanding. The key here is to choose your words carefully. The more precise and descriptive your text prompt is, the more accurate and relevant your generated image will be. For instance, if you want an AI model to generate a picture of a red rose, you might provide it with a prompt such as "a beautiful red rose blooming in the garden". The more specific your description is, the better chances are that you'll get what you're looking for. Lastly, try experimenting with different sentence structures when using text prompts. You may find that altering sentence structure can produce completely different results while utilizing the same keywords.

Experiment with Different AI Tools

Artificial Intelligence has given artists the ability to explore new creative avenues and push the boundaries of traditional art. The benefits of using AI in artwork are countless, from creating new visual styles to automating repetitive tasks. However, diving into this world can be overwhelming, especially when it comes to choosing which tools to use. Experimentation is key when it comes to exploring the potential of AI in art. There are many different programs available, each with its unique capabilities and limitations. Trying out multiple options will help you find the perfect tool for your specific needs.

One of the most exciting techniques for using AI in art is neural style transfer. This method applies a specific artistic style to an image or video by transferring its "style" onto a target image while maintaining its content structure. The result is a unique blend that combines both styles seamlessly. Generative Adversarial Networks (GANs) are another powerful tool that can create highly realistic images and videos through machine learning algorithms. GANs use two neural networks, one generating fake data and another evaluating it until it reaches a level that cannot be differentiated from real images or videos.

Deep dream algorithms can create surrealistic images through deep learning models by enhancing specific features within an image while suppressing others. When experimenting with these tools, don't be afraid to combine techniques creatively to achieve your desired effect. For example, combining neural style transfer with deep dream algorithms could produce mesmerizing visuals that have never been seen before. It's also worth mentioning that some AI tools require technical expertise and computational power beyond what a regular computer can handle without specialized hardware or software support. In such cases, cloud-based solutions like Google Colab or Amazon Web Services provide accessible solutions for creating stunning AI-generated art without breaking the bank on hardware costs.

Using Style Transfer Techniques

Artists have always found inspiration in the world around them, and technology has opened up new avenues for creative expression. AI-generated art has become increasingly popular in recent years, and many artists have been experimenting with different AI tools to create stunning works of art. One such tool is style transfer software, which allows artists to apply different styles to their artwork. Whether you're looking to create a surreal landscape or a portrait that resembles a famous artist's work, style transfer software can help you achieve your artistic vision.

The first step in using style transfer software is to find the right program for your needs. There are many different options available, each with its own strengths and weaknesses. Some popular programs include DeepArt.io, Prisma, and NeuralStyler. Once you've chosen a program, it's time to start experimenting with different styles. Style transfer software uses neural networks to analyze an image and extract its features before applying them to another image. This process can take anywhere from a few seconds to several minutes depending on the complexity of the images involved. To use style transfer software effectively, it's important to choose images that are compatible with each other. For example, if you're trying to apply a Van Gogh-style filter to a landscape photo, you'll want to choose an image with similar colors and textures as Van Gogh's paintings.

When using style transfer software, it's important not to be afraid of experimentation. Try out different filters and settings until you find the right combination that brings your artistic vision to life. One unique feature of style transfer software is its ability to mix multiple styles together. This allows artists to create truly unique works of art that combine elements from different genres or periods in art history. Another advantage of using style transfer software is its ability to save time while still producing high-quality artwork. Rather than spending hours painting or drawing by hand, artists can use style transfer software to achieve similar results in a fraction of the time.

Mastering Midjourney

As AI-generated art becomes increasingly popular, artists are constantly searching for ways to push the boundaries and create stunning pieces that stand out from the crowd. One tool that has gained popularity in recent years is Midjourney, which allows artists to create unique and visually striking images with the help of artificial intelligence. Midjourney is an AI-powered tool that uses a combination of machine learning algorithms and neural networks to generate complex patterns and shapes. Its main purpose is to help artists create stunning visual effects, such as fractals or psychedelic patterns. However, it can also be used for a variety of other purposes, including creating abstract art or even designing textiles.

One of the most significant benefits of using Midjourney is its flexibility. The program offers a wide range of customization options, allowing users to tweak various parameters such as color balance, scale, density, and more. This means that artists can easily adjust their creations until they achieve the desired effect. To get started with Midjourney, you will need to open up the program and select your desired parameters. You can then start experimenting by adjusting different settings until you find something that works for your artwork. It's important to keep in mind that Midjourney is an experimental tool - don't be afraid to try out different combinations until you find something that works.

One useful feature of Midjourney is its ability to generate random patterns based on certain parameters. This means that even if you aren't sure what kind of effect you want, you can simply hit "randomize" and see what comes up. This can be a great way to spark creativity and come up with new ideas for your artwork. Another way to use Midjourney effectively is by combining it with other tools or techniques. For example, you could use style transfer software (as discussed later) along with Midjourney to create even more unique and visually striking pieces. By experimenting with different combinations, you can create truly one-of-a-kind artwork that stands out from the crowd.

Dall-E - The Ultimate Tool for Creating Unique Art Pieces

As the world of artificial intelligence continues to evolve, we are constantly discovering new and exciting ways to harness its power for creating unique and visually stunning artwork. One such tool that has been making waves in the art community is Dall-E, a cutting-edge program that allows artists to create highly individualized pieces that stand out from the crowd. At its core, Dall-E is designed to generate images based on text input. This means that an artist can simply type in a description of what they want their image to look like, and Dall-E will use its advanced algorithms to create a completely original piece based on those specifications.

But what really sets Dall-E apart from other AI tools is its ability to think outside the box when it comes to generating images. Unlike other programs that may simply replicate existing styles or patterns, Dall-E has been trained on a massive dataset of diverse images, allowing it to generate truly unique visuals that are unlike anything you've ever seen before. One of the key features of Dall-E is its ability to understand context and nuance when interpreting text input. For example, if an artist were to type in "a red chair with curved legs," Dall-E would be able to generate an image based not just on the individual words themselves but also on their relationship with one another within the sentence. This means that artists can get incredibly specific about what they want their image to look like without having to worry about getting bogged down in technical details or jargon.

Of course, like any tool worth using, there is a learning curve involved when it comes to mastering Dall-E. But with practice and experimentation, artists can quickly become adept at using this powerful program for creating one-of-a-kind artwork. One tip for getting started with Dall-E is simply playing around with different types of inputs and seeing what the program generates. Try typing in descriptions of everyday objects or scenes and see how Dall-E interprets them. You may be surprised at the unique images that are generated!

Another trick for using Dall-E effectively is to think outside the box when it comes to your text input. Instead of simply describing what you want your image to look like, try incorporating more abstract concepts or emotions into your descriptions. This can lead to some truly fascinating and unexpected results. Ultimately, the key to creating stunning artwork with Dall-E is experimentation and a willingness to explore new possibilities. With its advanced algorithms and ability to generate truly unique visuals, this tool has quickly become a favorite among artists looking for a way to stand out from the crowd.

Understanding Diffusion Algorithm

Artists and designers are constantly seeking new ways to create visually appealing works of art. With the rise of artificial intelligence (AI), many have turned to using AI algorithms in their creative process. One such algorithm is the diffusion algorithm, which has gained popularity for its ability to generate stunning textures, colors, and elements for artwork. The diffusion algorithm is a mathematical model that simulates the movement of molecules in a liquid or gas. In the context of creating art, this algorithm can be used to simulate how colors diffuse or spread across a canvas. By manipulating different parameters such as time and space, artists can create unique patterns and effects for their artwork.

To effectively use the diffusion algorithm in your creations, it's important to understand its role in generating visually appealing textures and elements. The first step is to select an image that you want to apply the diffusion effect on. This could be anything from a landscape photograph to an abstract painting. Once you have your image selected, it's time to start experimenting with different parameters such as time steps and spatial scales. These parameters will affect how the colors spread across your canvas, creating unique patterns and effects.

One way to experiment with these parameters is by using software tools specifically designed for applying diffusion effects on images. These tools allow you to adjust various settings in real-time while previewing what the final result will look like. In addition to experimenting with different parameters, it's also important to consider how you want your final artwork to look like. Do you want a more organic or geometric feel? Do you want bright or muted colors? By having a clear vision of what you want your final artwork to look like, you can better tailor your use of the diffusion algorithm toward achieving that vision. Another useful technique when using the diffusion algorithm is combining it with other AI algorithms such as neural style transfer or GANs (Generative Adversarial Networks). By combining these algorithms, you can create even more unique and stunning works of art that stand out from the crowd.

Using Negative Prompts to Create Beautiful AI Art

"Art is the lie that tells the truth." - Pablo Picasso

As an artist, you know that inspiration can come from anywhere. But what about when you want to create something truly unique? Something that breaks the mold and pushes boundaries? That's where negative prompts come in. Negative prompts are prompts that tell your AI what not to do. By giving your model constraints on what it should avoid, you can encourage it to take risks and try new things. It's like telling a rebellious teenager not to do something - they'll probably be even more motivated to do it!

So why use negative prompts? For starters, they can help you break out of creative ruts. If you've been making art with the same techniques and styles for a while, negative prompts can shake things up and get your creative juices flowing again. Negative prompts can also help you create art that stands out from the crowd. By avoiding common themes or techniques, your AI-generated art will be truly one-of-a-kind.

But when should you use negative prompts? The answer is simple: whenever you want! There's no right or wrong time to use them - it all depends on your goals as an artist.

Let's take a look at some examples of negative prompts combined with main prompts:

EXAMPLE 1

- **Main prompt:** *"Create an image of a sunset over water."*
- **Negative prompt:** *"Do not use orange or red in the sky."*

Result: The AI-generated image features a stunning purple and blue sky with reflections in the water.

EXAMPLE 2

- **Main prompt:** *"Generate an abstract pattern using circles."*
- **Negative prompt:** *"Avoid using black."*

Result: The resulting image features bright colors and interesting shapes without relying on typical black lines.

EXAMPLE 3

- **Main prompt:** *"Create a portrait of a smiling woman."*
- **Negative prompt:** *"Do not include any teeth in the smile."*

Result: The AI-generated portrait features a unique closed-mouth smile, making it stand out from typical toothy grins.

ADVANCED EXAMPLE 1

- **Main prompt:** *"Teenage artist creating digital art on computer."*
- **Negative prompt:** (None used)

Result:

AI-generated art created with no negative prompt. Notice the extra finger on the right hand.

ADVANCED EXAMPLE 2

- **Main prompt:** *"Teenage artist creating digital art on computer."*

- **Negative prompt:** *"Close up, two heads, two faces, plastic, Deformed, blurry, bad anatomy, bad eyes, crossed eyes, disfigured, poorly drawn face, mutation, mutated, ((extra limb)), ugly, poorly drawn hands, missing limb, blurry, floating limbs, disconnected limbs, malformed hands, blur, out of focus, long neck, long body, ((((mutated hands and fingers)))), (((out of frame))),, extra fingers"*

Result:

AI-generated art using main and negative prompts.

As you can see, negative prompts can lead to some truly stunning and unexpected results. But it's important to remember that they're not a magic solution - you still need to have a strong main prompt and a well-trained model to get the best results. You can experiment with negative prompts until you get the desired result. Incorporating negative prompts into your AI-generated art practice can be just the thing you need to take your work to the next level. So go ahead - break some rules, try something new, and see where your creativity takes you!

By following these tips and tricks, you'll be able to create stunning pieces of art using artificial intelligence while pushing yourself creatively further than ever before!

COMMON MISTAKES TO AVOID

Avoid Over-training

One common mistake made while creating AI-generated artwork is over-training on a particular dataset or model. Over-training leads to loss in diversity within generated images as well as less variety between iterations produced by artistic models based on non-AI methods. It would be best if you always kept in mind that creating art is not about generating perfect images. There is a beauty in imperfection, and the same goes for AI-generated artwork. It's essential to know when to stop training the system and assess the artwork it has generated so far. Begin with considering experimenting with different datasets or models and look out for new or under-optimized ones. Use transfer learning as another approach to create unique datasets as well.

Avoid Prolonged Sessions

In creating AI-generated art, it can be easy to get swept away in the excitement of seeing what the neural network will produce. It can be tempting to let the algorithm run indefinitely, hoping that it will eventually create something truly remarkable. However, as with any creative process, it is essential to know when to stop and evaluate what has been produced so far. One way to approach this is by setting specific goals for the artwork you want to create. Are you looking for a particular aesthetic or style? Do you have a specific subject or theme in mind? By defining clear objectives at the outset, you can avoid getting lost in an endless cycle of experimentation without purpose.

Another way to manage the mid-journey of AI-generated art is by keeping a record of each iteration. Each time you run your algorithm with new settings or data inputs, save the output as a separate file. Then take some time to compare each version and identify which ones are moving closer towards your goals and which are not. This approach allows you to track your progress and adjust your course as needed. Finally, don't be afraid to step back from your work periodically and take a break. Sometimes our minds need time away from a project before we can see it with fresh eyes and gain new insights into what we want it to become. Giving yourself space during the middle of creating AI-generated art can lead to breakthroughs in creativity that wouldn't have been possible otherwise.

Over-reliance on AI Algorithms

A common mistake made by artists new to AI-generated art is an over-reliance on algorithms. While these algorithms are incredibly powerful, they should not be seen as a replacement for artistic intuition and creativity. Instead, they should be seen as tools that can be used in conjunction with the artist's own vision to create something truly unique. To avoid falling into the trap of over-reliance on algorithms, it's important for artists to understand how these algorithms work and what their limitations are. This can help artists use them effectively without sacrificing their own creative vision.

Ignoring the Importance of Post-Processing

Another mistake that many artists make when creating AI-generated art is ignoring the importance of post-processing. While the initial output from an algorithm may be impressive, it's often necessary to make further adjustments and edits to achieve a truly polished final product. Post-processing can involve everything from adjusting colors and contrast levels to cropping or resizing an image. By taking the time to fine-tune their creations in this way, artists will be able to produce pieces of art that truly stand out from the crowd.

Failing to Experiment with Different Algorithms

A third common mistake made by artists working with AI-generated art is failing to experiment with different algorithms. While certain algorithms may work well for certain styles or types of artwork, others may produce unexpected or interesting results when used in new ways. By experimenting with different algorithms, artists can discover new techniques and approaches that they may not have thought of otherwise. This can lead to exciting breakthroughs in their art and open up new avenues for exploration.

Not Pushing the Limits of AI Technology

Finally, artists may be too cautious or hesitant when it comes to pushing the limits of AI technology. While it's important to be mindful of ethical considerations and other concerns, this should not prevent artists from exploring all the creative possibilities that AI-generated art has to offer. By pushing the limits of what is currently possible with AI technology, artists can create truly groundbreaking work that pushes the boundaries of what we think of as "art." This can help them stand out in a crowded field and make a lasting impact on the art world.

Chapter Nine

Training Your AI Tools

TRAINING YOUR OWN NEURAL NETWORK

Neural networks are the backbone of artificial intelligence. They are a set of algorithms that allow machines to learn by recognizing patterns in data, just like humans do. Training your own neural network gives you greater control over the output and enables you to create unique solutions tailored to your specific needs. The first step in training a neural network is selecting an appropriate dataset. The dataset should include a wide variety of examples that represent the problem you want to solve. For example, if you want to train a network to recognize faces, your dataset should include images with different poses, ages, and backgrounds. You should also ensure that your dataset is large enough for the model to learn from and generalize well. Once you have selected your dataset, it's time to choose an appropriate algorithm. There are many different types of algorithms available for training neural networks, each with its strengths and weaknesses. Some popular options include convolutional neural networks (CNNs) for image recognition tasks and recurrent neural networks (RNNs) for natural language processing.

After selecting an algorithm, it's important to optimize the model parameters for best performance. These parameters include learning rate, batch size, and optimization function among others which impact how quickly or slowly the model learns from data. Hyperparameter tuning techniques can be used here such as Grid Search or Random Search which help explore various combinations of parameter values. Finally, it's essential to evaluate how well your model performs by testing with new data not seen during training process known as a validation set. This helps prevent overfitting where the network becomes too good at recognizing examples shown during training but fails when presented with new data such as real-world scenarios.

TRAINING YOUR AI ART GENERATORS

Artists have always had a unique way of expressing themselves through their artwork. Every artist has their own style, which they hone over time. However, what if an artist could create art that is uniquely theirs, but with the help of artificial intelligence? This is where AI art generators come in. AI art generators use machine learning algorithms to generate original pieces of art. By using images created by the artist as training data for the algorithm, it can then generate new pieces that reflect the artist's style. In this chapter, we will explore different approaches to creating custom training datasets for AI-art generation and provide tips for optimizing your model's output.

Creating a Custom Dataset

The beauty of neural networks and AI-art generators lies in their ability to learn and adapt from data. As such, it's crucial to have a well-curated dataset that meets your specific needs if you want to achieve the best results. The first step in training your AI-art generator is to create a custom dataset. This involves collecting images of your own artwork and organizing them into a format that can be used by the algorithm. When creating a custom dataset for AI-art generation, it's important to choose high-quality images that capture your unique style. These images will form the basis of your training data and will influence the output of your model. Once you have collected your images, you will need to organize them into folders based on their respective categories. For example, if you're creating an AI-art generator that generates landscape paintings, you might want to categorize each image based on its location or subject matter.

Defining Your Dataset

The first step in creating a custom dataset is defining what you want it to accomplish. Determine the type of output you're hoping to achieve, as this will guide the types of data you'll need to include. For example, if you're training an AI-art generator, perhaps you want it to produce paintings in the style of Van Gogh. In this case, images of Van Gogh's artwork would be an essential part of your dataset.

Organizing Data

With all this data at hand, organizing them becomes critical; otherwise, they'll be difficult or impossible for your neural network or AI-art generator algorithm to work with effectively. Start by labeling each piece of data with relevant information such as artist name or painting title. Additionally, organize these labeled images into subfolders based on their similarities - grouping them by style or color palette can help ensure that related pieces are easily accessible when needed.

Optimizing Your Model's Output

After creating your custom dataset, it's time to train your model using an appropriate algorithm such as generative adversarial networks (GANs) or autoencoders. When training your model, there are several parameters that can be fine-tuned in order to optimize its output. These include regularization parameters and learning rates among others. higher-qualityRegularization parameters are used to prevent overfitting by penalizing complex models while learning rates affect how quickly or slowly the network adapts during training which affects convergence speed. By carefully adjusting these parameters, you can achieve higher quality output from your AI-art generator.

Fine-Tuning Your Output

Even after training your model with a custom dataset and optimizing its parameters, there may still be room for improvement in the final output. This is where advanced techniques like transfer learning or ensemble modeling come in. Transfer learning involves taking a pre-trained model and tweaking it for your specific use case, while ensemble modeling uses multiple models to produce more accurate results. These techniques can help fine-tune the output of your AI-art generator even further.

ETHICAL CONSIDERATIONS

Ethical issues with AI art were mentioned previously in this book and are worth repeating as artists train their AI tools. As we delve deeper into the world of Neural Networks and AI Art Generators, it's important to address the ethical considerations surrounding their use. While these technologies are undoubtedly exciting and revolutionary, they also raise some complex **ethical questions** that must be taken seriously. One of the most significant concerns in this regard is copyright issues. It's imperative that we don't steal the work of other artists to train our networks or generate new art. This is not only unethical but also illegal, and could potentially result in legal action being taken against you.

To avoid any such problems, it's recommended that **you only use images that are your art, or that you own or have obtained copyright permission for**. This may require some extra effort on your part, but it's essential if you want to stay on the right side of the law and maintain your integrity as an artist. Another issue to consider is whether using AI-generated art created by others for commercial purposes is ethical. While there may be no legal barriers preventing you from doing so, some may argue that profiting from someone else's creation in this way is morally questionable. Of course, this is a complex topic with no easy answers. Some argue that using AI-generated art can actually benefit artists by inspiring them with new ideas and techniques they might not have otherwise considered. Others contend that it detracts from the value of original artistic expression and undermines creativity.Ultimately, each artist must decide for themselves what they feel comfortable with in terms of using AI-generated art for commercial purposes. However, it's important to consider carefully how your actions will impact other artists working in this field.

Finally, we need to address the issue of **bias** when training neural networks on images or data sets representing certain groups or demographics. For example, if a network is trained primarily on images of white people or white-dominated cultures, it may struggle when presented with images featuring people from other racial backgrounds. This bias can be particularly problematic in areas such as facial recognition and criminal justice, where the consequences of inaccurate or discriminatory algorithms can be severe. As such, it's essential that we take steps to ensure our networks are trained on diverse data sets that represent a broad range of cultural backgrounds and perspectives.

In conclusion, while the world of Neural Networks and AI Art Generators is undoubtedly exciting, we must approach it with caution and sensitivity to the ethical considerations involved. By taking these issues seriously and striving to use these technologies responsibly, we can leverage their potential to create new forms of artistic expression while minimizing harm to others. Besides, as an artist, it is honorable to leave your own fingerprint on the world without being a clone of someone else. There was only one Pablo Picasso, and one Vincent Van Gogh. They left their character and unique styles in their art. The world loved them for this. There is only one of you. Be yourself without being a clone of someone else. Give the world your unique spin in your art and life.

Chapter Ten

The Success Stories of Artists Who Have Embraced AI

The digital age has transformed the way we create and consume art. Today, artists are experimenting with new mediums and techniques to produce stunning works that challenge traditional notions of what constitutes art. One such medium that has been gaining popularity in recent years is AI-generated art. Many artists have embraced AI as a tool to enhance their creative process and push the boundaries of their artwork. One notable success story is the British artist, **Anna Ridler**, whose AI-generated artwork "**Mosaic Virus**" was sold at Christie's for over $100,000. The artwork was created using machine learning algorithms that analyzed thousands of images of flowers to generate unique patterns and colors. Another artist who has embraced AI in her work is **Refik Anadol**. The Turkish-born artist combines artificial intelligence with data from urban environments to create immersive installations that explore the relationship between humans and technology. One of her most notable works is "**Melting Memories**," which uses machine learning algorithms to transform brainwave data into mesmerizing visualizations.

In addition to individual artists, there are also collectives that have formed around AI-generated art. One such collective is **Obvious**, a Paris-based group of friends who use generative adversarial networks (GANs) to create unique portraits and landscapes that blur the line between human creativity and machine intelligence. These artists' success stories highlight the potential of AI in unlocking new avenues for creative expression and pushing the limits of what we think is possible through traditional art forms. As more artists begin experimenting with AI technologies, we can expect to see even more groundbreaking artworks emerge in the future.

While Refik Anadol and Anna Ridler may have garnered much attention for their groundbreaking works, they are not the only ones in this field. In this chapter, we will explore some of the other successful AI artists who have made strides between 2021 and 2023. One such artist is **Trevor Paglen**, whose work "**Machine-Readable Hito**" uses facial recognition algorithms to analyze portraits by Japanese artist Hito Steyerl. Paglen's work examines how machines see and interpret human faces, raising questions about surveillance and privacy in the digital age. To create his work, he used custom machine-learning algorithms that he developed himself.

Another notable AI artist is **Sougwen Chung**, who has been exploring how humans can collaborate with machines to create art. Her project "**Drawing Operations**" involves a robotic arm that mimics her drawing movements on a wall-mounted canvas while also adding its own interpretations. The result is an intricate dance between human creativity and machine intelligence. In addition to these individual artists, there are also collectives making waves in the world of AI art. One such collective is DeepDreamVisionQuest, which includes members from diverse backgrounds such as computer science and fine arts. Their project "Dreams of Dali" uses deep learning algorithms to generate imagery inspired by Salvador Dali's works.

When it comes to tools used by these artists in their creations, there is no one-size-fits-all answer. Many use custom-built software or develop their own algorithms specific to their needs. Others may rely on off-the-shelf machine learning libraries like TensorFlow or PyTorch. The success stories of these artists show that AI has opened up new avenues for creative expression beyond what was previously thought possible. As we move forward into the future, it is exciting to think about what other innovative and boundary-pushing works these artists will come up with.

machine-learningBut what does this mean for traditional art forms? Will they be replaced by machines? It's unlikely. Instead, we'll see a shift in how artists approach their work – using technology as another tool at their disposal rather than replacing traditional methods entirely. In conclusion, artificial intelligence presents enormous potential for artists who want to push boundaries and experiment with new techniques. The success stories of Anna Ridler and Refik Anadol serve as inspiration for others looking to incorporate AI into their work. As we move forward into uncharted territory, it's exciting to imagine the possibilities that lie ahead.

Chapter Eleven

The Future Canvas: Envisioning AI's Impact on Art

The Future of AI in Art

As we continue to witness the rapid evolution of AI technology, it's natural to wonder how this will shape the future of artistic expression. The possibilities are endless, and in this chapter, we will explore some potential impacts on the wider world beyond just traditional artwork. One area where AI is already making a significant impact is in the realm of design. From fashion to product design, AI algorithms are being used to generate new and innovative ideas. In fact, many designers are already using AI tools to help them create more complex designs that would be impossible without machine assistance.

But what about art forms like painting or sculpture? Will these be replaced by machines? It's unlikely. While it's true that machines can create incredible works of art on their own, there will always be a place for human creativity in the arts. Instead, we're more likely to see artists using AI as an aid to push their creative boundaries even further. For example, an artist might use an AI tool to generate unique color palettes or suggest new compositions based on previous works. These tools could help artists explore new ideas and break free from creative ruts.

Another exciting possibility is the integration of virtual reality (VR) and augmented reality (AR) technology with AI-generated art. Imagine walking through a gallery filled with interactive installations that blend physical and digital elements seamlessly. With AR or VR technology guiding us through these spaces, we could experience art like never before. Of course, as with any emerging technology there are bound to be challenges along the way. One potential issue is the question of authenticity versus artificiality - when does a work created with the assistance of an algorithm cease being "art" and become something else entirely? This is something that artists will need to grapple with as they continue exploring new ways of using these tools.

Another challenge is ensuring that access to these technologies remains equitable across all communities. As AI continues to evolve, there is a risk that only those with the resources to invest in cutting-edge technology will be able to create truly innovative works of art. It's up to us as a society to ensure that everyone has access to these tools and the opportunities they bring. Despite these challenges, the future of AI in art is incredibly exciting. We're on the cusp of a new artistic revolution, one where human creativity and technological innovation work hand-in-hand to unlock new possibilities. Whether it's exploring new mediums, pushing creative boundaries or creating entirely new forms of art, the future looks bright for artists who embrace this emerging technology.

In conclusion, it's clear that AI will play an increasingly important role in shaping the future of artistic expression. While there are certainly challenges ahead, we must focus on embracing these new technologies and using them as an aid rather than replacement for human creativity. By doing so, we can unleash our imaginations and create a world filled with innovative and inspiring works of art that were previously unimaginable.

The Future is Bright

While there are certainly challenges and ethical considerations surrounding the use of AI in art, the future looks bright for those willing to embrace this new technology. With continued advancements in machine learning algorithms, we can expect to see even more impressive work created through collaboration between humans and machines. For those who are open to exploring new tools and techniques, AI has the potential to unlock a whole new realm of creative possibilities. The future of art may be powered by machines, but it will always be driven by human imagination.

Conclusion

In conclusion, AI art is revolutionizing the creative industry by providing artists with new and exciting ways to unleash their creativity. While there are certainly ethical implications to consider when working with AI-generated art, it is clear that this technology has the potential to produce stunning works of art that would not have been possible otherwise. As more and more artists begin to embrace AI as a tool in their artistic workflow, we can look forward to an even more diverse and innovative artistic landscape in the years ahead. One possibility for the future of generative AI art is a new era of collaboration between humans and machines. As AI artists become more advanced, they could work alongside human artists to create entirely new forms of art that blend both human creativity with machine intelligence. This collaboration could lead to new insights into creativity itself, as well as an entirely new artistic style that has yet to be explored or imagined.

As we look towards the future, it is clear that AI art will continue to push boundaries and redefine what it means to be creative. The possibilities are boundless, and we can only imagine what new forms of artistic expression will emerge in the years ahead. So let us appreciate and embrace this exciting new era of human ingenuity!

References

- Charny, D. (2020). The Rise of Artificial Intelligence in Art. Forbes.
- Colton, S., & Wiggins, G. A. (2012). Computational creativity: The final frontier?. In Proceedings of the 3rd International Conference on Computational Creativity (pp. 1-7).
- McCormack, J., & d'Inverno, M. (2012). Computers and creativity. Springer.
- Tanaka, A. (2018). Artificial Intelligence and Music. In Oxford Handbook of Algorithmic Music (pp. 479-495). Oxford University Press.
- Hassabis, D. (2019). AI at DeepMind and Its Potential for the Arts. In AI and Creativity (pp. 101-110). Springer.
- Ensmenger, N. (2019). Machine Learning and Data Science in the Age of Neo-Eugenics. In AI and Creativity (pp. 25-44). Springer.
- Gero, J. S. (2018). Creativity in the Age of Smart Machines. Leonardo, 51(2), 224-230.

- Fiebrink, R., & Wilkie, T. (2020). Live Interfaces for Music-making: Surveying the State of the Art. Computer Music Journal, 44(3), 13-32.

- Liao, C. H., & Lo, Y. J. (2019). A study on the effect of artificial intelligence on art creation process. Journal of Intelligent & Fuzzy Systems, 37(2), 2605-2616.

- Zhu, J. Y., Park, T., Isola, P., & Efros, A. A. (2017). Unpaired Image-to-Image Translation Using Cycle-Consistent Adversarial Networks. In Proceedings of the IEEE international conference on computer vision (pp. 2223-2232).

- Loke, L., & Khut, G. (2018). Creative AI and situated cognition: A case study in co-creativity. Digital Creativity, 29(1), 72-85.

- Johnson, M. (2020). The Robots Are Coming for Our Art Jobs. The New York Times Magazine, 19.

www.ingramcontent.com/pod-product-compliance
Ingram Content Group UK Ltd.
Pitfield, Milton Keynes, MK11 3LW, UK
UKHW040011200726
13854UKWH00001B/153

9 798215 672365